Let's Go to Stop Water Pollution

The whole earth depends on water. But the more our civilization has grown, the dirtier the water has become. You visit a water treatment plant to find out how our cities have to purify the water they use. You hope that our towns and factories learn how to keep sewage and oil and chemicals out of water so that it will not become polluted in the first place.

Let's Go to
Stop Water Pollution

by Michael Chester

illustrated by Albert Micale

G. P. Putnam's Sons   New York

The author and the artist wish to thank the following for their
help in the preparation of this book: Judi Eckhardt and Harry
Sanders of the San Jose-Santa Clara Water Pollution Control
Plant; Fred Williams of the Rinconada Water Treatment Plant;
The Lauman Company, Bethpage, N.Y.

You are coming to the end of a camping trip. You are lying by the edge of a mountain stream, listening to the soft, ringing sound of the water as it runs over the rocks. Small ripples and whirlpools form near the edge of the stream among the mossy rocks. Once in a while a stick or a leaf floats past. Through the clear water you can see the pebbles and sand grains at the bottom of the stream. You kneel to drink from the stream. The water is fresh and cool.

54444

Resting beside this mountain stream, you get the feeling that water is one of the cleanest and most beautiful things in the world.

Hours later, on your way back to town, you watch the stream widen and deepen until it becomes a river. The broad river looks beautiful from the distance. But when you go to walk along its banks, you see that the water is not very clean here. Instead, it looks murky and scummy.

You see a man crouching to examine some fish that are lying on the ground. At first you think that he is a fisherman looking at his catch. Then you talk to him and find out that he is a ranger, whose job it is to watch over fish and animal life. The fish that he is looking at were washed up along the bank — dead. The ranger shakes his head as he studies the fish. "There's probably something in this water that's killing them."

"What would do that?" you ask.

"Oh, it's hard to say. Several things could cause it. Insecticides might have mixed with the river water in irrigation ditches of some farms near here. Or sewage may have leaked out of cesspools and been carried into the river during a heavy rain. Different kinds of chemicals and detergents

get dumped into rivers sometimes, too. All these things can kill fish and ducks. Of course, this is a small fish kill. In big fish kills, thousands of fish are destroyed — or even millions."

"That would really be bad," you say.

"Yes, and it's getting bad in general," says the ranger. "If this goes on, there won't be any more fish in this river. The water is getting so full of poisons and sewage that fishing could be ruined in this whole area. And it's even worse near the city, where the chemicals are pouring into the river by the millions of gallons. There the river is really dirty."

That night you sleep in a motel near the river. You can hear the water flowing in the distance, and looking out the window of the motel, you can see the reflection of lights from towns across the river. The river looks beautiful now, and you think about how long it has flowed between these banks and about how many boats have traveled on it. It is hard to believe that this great old river is being ruined.

The next morning you are going to see how the towns near the river use the river water for drinking. At first the idea sounds terrible to you. Would anyone drink the water from the river, all full of chemicals and sewage and dead fish and dead ducks?

There is a small dam in the river just downstream from the motel. The water that collects on the upstream side of the dam acts as a reservoir to supply water to nearby towns. This water flows through concrete canals called aqueducts. You follow an aqueduct westward from the dam, across the countryside, through woods and farmlands and small country villages. Watching the aqueduct from the window of the car, you see that the water is greenish and has logs and boards floating in it. It certainly doesn't look like drinking water.

Finally, you come to a small range of hills. There the aqueduct enters a large underground pipeline that goes under the hills. But the road that you are following goes upward, over the range. When you reach the crest, you look back in the direction that you came. In the distance you see a long, winding ribbon of water — it is the river, and it looks like a band of light or a snake with silvery scales.

Then you look westward. At the foot of the hills you see a group of tanks and reservoirs, some of them circular in shape, others rectangular. You are looking down at a water treatment plant that is being fed by the underground pipeline. There the river water is being cleaned before supplying the nearby towns.

At the treatment plant you meet a man, named Mr. Pinto, who shows you around. You follow him along concrete walkways past the edges of open tanks. The tanks look like shallow ponds with fences around them. Then you see one of the tanks that is empty. It is very deep, and as you look far down into it, you see why these tanks need to be fenced. They certainly are not the shallow pools that they seem to be.

"These tanks are the settling tanks," says Mr. Pinto. Then he explains the way that the water is cleaned. Before the water from the aqueduct comes into the settling tanks, it flows through screens. The screens take large objects, such as logs, shoes, dead fish, and walnuts out of the water.

But even with all of these objects screened out, the water is still dirty. In the settling tanks, chemicals called coagulants are added to the water. These chemicals mix with the mud and silt to form a sticky material called floc. In the settling tanks the floc settles to the bottom. Automatic mechanical scrapers slowly move across the bottom of the tanks to scrape the floc into drains. You cannot see the scrapers at work because the water is still too green to see through. But looking down into the one empty tank, you can see the big metal scraping arms.

"The screens and the settling tanks together are called primary treatment," says Mr. Pinto. "Many towns have that and nothing else. Screens, settling tanks, and

then the water goes into the city pipes for drinking." He shakes his head sadly.

"Do you do more things to clean the water then?" you ask.

Mr. Pinto nods. "We certainly do. We have secondary treatment, too. I'll show you."

You follow him to the next row of tanks. The water there looks much cleaner because it has already gone through the settling tanks. "But it's not as clean as it looks," says Mr. Pinto. "There is still pollution in the water. The secondary treatment happens at the bottom of these filtering tanks. See how sandy the bottom is?"

Looking down into the deep tank through water that is still a little cloudy, you can barely see the sandy bottom of the tank.

Mr. Pinto explains that the layer of sand is two or three feet deep all over the bottom of the tank. Underneath the sand is a layer of gravel that is another two or three feet deep, and there are pipes sticking up into the gravel to collect the water. So all the water gets filtered through the sand before it goes into the pipes. Small particles, various bacteria, and algae — the microscopic plant life that makes the water green — are filtered out as the water goes through the sand.

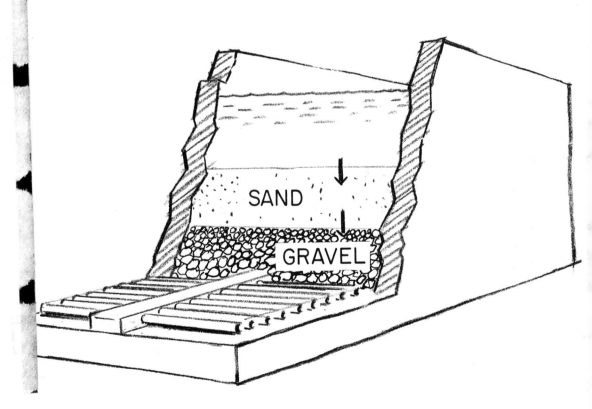

"Doesn't the sand get dirty after a while?" you ask.

"Right," says Mr. Pinto. "All the pollution finally forms a jellylike layer in the sand. But every once in a while we reverse the flow of water and let the water squirt up through the gravel and sand. That washes the jellylike layer off, and it is circulated back through the settling tanks, where it settles to the bottom with the floc."

"Where does the water go after it leaves the filtering tanks?"

Mr. Pinto points toward a circular reservoir just past the long row of filtering tanks. "The pipes at the bottom take it to that reservoir over there. And there we add chlorine salts to kill off bacteria that are left."

"That sounds pretty good," you say. "But sometimes I don't like the way water tastes after it has chlorine in it."

Mr. Pinto tells you that some towns get rid of much of the chlorine taste by using a spray system. The air from the treatment plant is sprayed out of big fountains. Air mixes into the fine spray, and some of the chlorinated taste is taken away.

Then Mr. Pinto takes you into the nearby building where he works. There you see a control room full of valves and gauges. By turning the valves, Mr. Pinto and the people who work with him can control the flow of water. Tanks can be emptied for repair or cleaning, or the water flow can be reversed in the filtering tanks. Mr. Pinto shows you a sink with two faucets. He opens one of the faucets, and greenish water comes out — that is aqueduct water, before it has had treatment. Then he opens the other faucet, and clear water comes out — water that has had primary treatment in the settling tanks, secondary treatment in the filtering tanks, and the chlorination. He

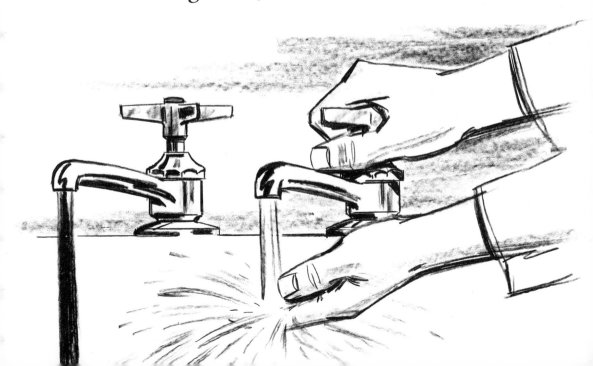

also shows you a laboratory where scientists are testing samples of the water to see if any polluting chemicals or certain kinds of bacteria are in the clear water. In this way the scientists can check to see if the treatment is really getting the water clean.

As you leave the building, you see a row of large rectangular troughs. Those are floc lagoons, where the floc is piped from the settling tanks. The floc dries out in the lagoons and then is taken away in trucks to be used as fertilizer on farms.

Mr. Pinto walks with you to your car. "It's too bad," says Mr. Pinto, "that more isn't done to keep sewage and chemicals out of the river water to begin with. We don't do enough of that. The result is more work for people downstream. They have to clean the water all over again. The trouble is that people worry more about cleaning their own water than they do about cleaning the water that goes downstream to other people."

After you leave the treatment plant and travel back to the river and travel downstream along its banks, you see more of what Mr. Pinto meant. The river gets dirtier and dirtier as you go toward the sea. Even though the cities up the coast are cleaning their drinking water, they are not

being careful about sewage and insecticides that flow back into the river. The river is carrying all this pollution, and the water looks dark and murky now, even in the distance.

As you drive, you see the countryside change into an industrial area. You pass a chemical factory, where you see a flood of bubbling chemicals being poured into the river from a big pipe. These are waste chemicals, and the chemical company is getting rid of them by pouring them into the river. The river will carry them out to sea.

But along the way these chemicals will make trouble. You notice that the water is a different color where the chemicals are pouring in, and the surface looks oily.

Finally, you come to the estuary — the place where the polluted river flows into the bay. But the waters of the river are not the only source of pollution that empties into the bay. Oils and chemicals and sewage have been dumped directly into the bay by factories, ships, and sewage systems. The sand that you see along the shore is full of oil and tar, and the smell of foul waters is everywhere.

You visit the water pollution control offices, where people are working to prevent water pollution. A woman named Mrs. Deasy, who works there, takes you on a

journey along the coast. She shows you
the way that filled-in land juts out into the
bay and blocks the natural flow of water
out to sea, trapping the pollution inside the
bay.

She also shows you the deserted fish canneries. The fish and the clams and oysters that used to be plentiful in the bay are almost all gone, and the fisheries have gone out of business. "Nothing could live in these waters," says Mrs. Deasy. "It isn't even much good for boating anymore, and nobody in his right mind would swim here." She points to a sign on the shore that reads:

THIS BEACH IS CLOSED BY ORDER OF THE BOARD OF HEALTH... NO SWIMMING ALLOWED.

"But we are doing things," says Mrs. Deasy. "Would you like to see some of our work?"

You go with Mrs. Deasy to a sewage treatment plant by the bay. You notice how, in many ways, it looks like the water treatment plant. Here, too, are rows of fenced tanks separated by concrete walkways.

But there are several differences in the way this plant operates. First, the sewage water coming in from large sewage pipes is chlorinated to lessen its smell. The smell of sewage and chlorine together is odd and unpleasant — as you find out when you walk past the tanks — but it is not nearly as bad as the sewage alone would be.

After chlorination, the sewage water flows through screens and grit-removal tanks.

INCLINED SCREW FOR REMOVING GRIT

Standing near these tanks, you see the rotating metal fins that take hard objects, such as sticks and fruit pits, out of the sewage.

Mrs. Deasy peers into a bin where the grit is dropped out. "You can tell what kind of fruit canning is going on now by looking at pits here. It looks as if apricot canning is the main thing now." Looking in the bin, you also see many apricot pits.

From the grit tanks the water flows into settling tanks very much like those at the water treatment plant. The floc that settles to the bottoms of these tanks is called raw sludge. Mrs. Deasy explains that the sludge is used as an important part of the sewage treatment. She shows you the next row of tanks. These are aeration tanks. The sew-

age water and the raw sludge are pumped
into these tanks, where the muddy sludge
bubbles and swirls around.

"Air is being forced into the sludge here," says Mrs. Deasy, "and now it is called activated sludge. Without the air, the bacteria in the sludge would digest the sewage slowly, and the gases that they would give off would smell awful. But the air allows the bacteria in the activated sludge to grow rapidly and to digest sewage very well. The gases that are given off are odorless, and all the sewage in the water is digested and done away with. Then the water is allowed to flow back into the bay."

"You mean the bacteria do the cleaning work for you?"

Mrs. Deasy smiles. "Yes. They're the best workers we have. Of course, they don't know it."

"Is the water really clean by that time?" you ask.

"Pretty clean," she says. "I'll show you proof of that." She takes you into a chemical laboratory where the water is tested. There she shows you a tank of live fish. "Those fish are swimming in the treated water. We keep records of how many of the fish stay alive. If they do pretty well,

then we know that the treated water can be discharged into the bay without destroying the living things there. This is a new plant. But in a few years we will be handling sewage from the whole area. Life will start to come back into this bay, and the good smell of salt air will return, too."

"What happens to the sludge after it's used for digesting the sewage?" you ask.

Mrs. Deasy explains that after the activated sludge is separated from the treated water, some of it is pumped back into the aeration tanks to be used again. Any extra sludge is concentrated into a thick mixture and pumped into digesters. She takes you outside again and shows you high, round tanks as big as buildings. They are the digesters. "In there," says Mrs. Deasy, "the

GAS OUTLET

SLUDGE
OUTLET

sludge is digested by its own bacteria, without air. A lot of natural gas is given off, and it's burnable, so it is pumped out of the closed digesters and used to run the pumps and generators and air blowers of the plant. So, you see, we are putting our bacteria to work for us again. They run our machinery for us. Then, the half-dried digested sludge is taken from the digesters by truck and dumped into the sludge lagoons across the road, where it dries out some more."

"That reminds me of the floc lagoons at the water treatment plant," you say.

"It's the same sort of thing," agrees Mrs. Deasy. "The sludge lagoons produce an even richer fertilizer, though."

Then Mrs. Deasy says that sewage treatment takes care of a big part of the water pollution problem. She talks about other steps that are being taken, such as the way that most chemical companies are treating harmful chemicals before dumping them into the water. But more things have to be done, such as keeping oil out of the bay waters. Mrs. Deasy mentions the oil tanker that was in the headlines a few years ago when it was wrecked in the English Channel and poured millions of gallons of oil into the water, killing the shore creatures and ruining good beaches for miles along the coast.

"Is water pollution a very serious problem?" you ask. "As serious as war and being poor and that kind of thing?"

Mrs. Deasy nods and frowns. "Very serious. We drink water; we bathe in it; we grow our crops and feed our livestock with it; we run our factories with it. The whole earth depends on water. But that water is being polluted more and more. The more our civilization has grown, the dirtier the water has become. But this water means life. We can't go on ruining it."

Looking out at the bay and at the estuary where the river winds its way into the bay, you think that she must be right.

You remember the beautiful stream in the mountains, and you think of the great river and how proudly it flows. And you think of the bay — how it looks at night with lights reflected in the water. And you think of the wide-open sea and of clean beaches with white sand. And you think of a boat ride you took once and of good times you have had swimming. You think of the taste of a cold glass of water on a hot summer day when you're very thirsty. And then you know how much you would like to see the river and the bay and all the life-giving waters made clean again.

Glossary

ACTIVATED SLUDGE — sludge that has been aerated so that the bacteria in the sludge will digest sewage quickly and cleanly.

AERATION — getting air into water or sludge by a spraying or bubbling process.

ALGAE — microscopic plant life that gives water a green color.

AQUEDUCT — a canal or water line that carries water from a dam or reservoir to cities and towns.

BACTERIA — microscopic one-celled plant life — either harmful, causing disease, or helpful, as in digestion of sewage.

CHLORINATION — adding chlorine salts to water or sewage.

CHLORINE SALTS — chemicals added to water or sewage to help stop pollution.

COAGULANTS — chemicals that mix with mud, silt, and sewage to form floc.

DIGESTERS — large, closed tanks at a sewage treatment plant where leftover sludge is digested to produce natural gas and half-dried sludge.

ESTUARY — where a river empties into a bay or sea.

FILTERING TANK — a tank in which water is cleaned by flowing through a layer of sand.

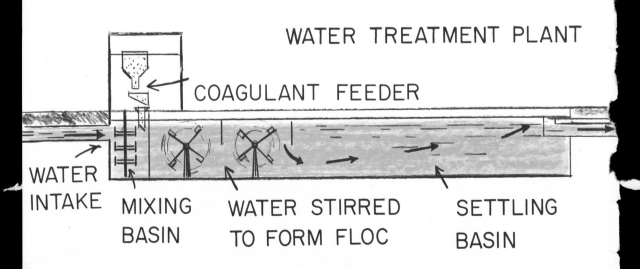

WATER TREATMENT PLANT

COAGULANT FEEDER

WATER INTAKE   MIXING BASIN   WATER STIRRED TO FORM FLOC   SETTLING BASIN

FISH KILL — the death of large numbers of fish because of water pollution.

FLOC — a sticky material that settles to the bottom of a tank when water is cleaned.

INSECTICIDE — chemicals used to poison insects.

LAGOON — usually a body of salt water surrounded by land, but, in connection with water pollution, a trough where floc or sludge is dried.

NATURAL GAS — a gas given off by decaying matter which is used as a fuel.

PRIMARY TREATMENT — the cleaning of water by passing it through a screen and by removing the floc in a settling tank.

RESERVOIR — a place where drinking water is stored.

SECONDARY TREATMENT — the filtering of drinking water through sand.

SETTLING TANK — where floc or sludge is taken out of water.

SEWAGE TREATMENT PLANT — a place where water is treated before being poured into a bay or sea.

SILT — a very fine soil carried by river water.

SLUDGE — a thick, muddy floc.

WATER TREATMENT PLANT — a place where water is treated before being piped to homes.

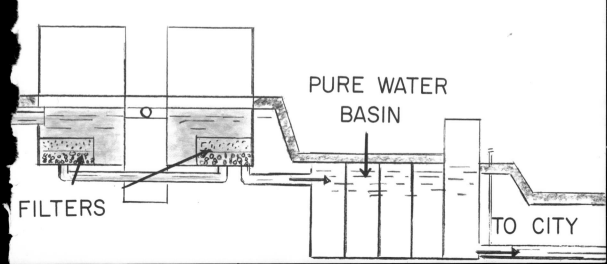

FILTERS

PURE WATER BASIN

TO CITY

Other Things to Do While Reading
Let's Go to Stop Water Pollution

1. Visit the waterworks in your town or city to see its primary and secondary treatment for the water you drink.
2. Take a walk along the nearest river or lake in your area. What signs of pollution do you see? What signs of animal life do you see? What does the presence of fish or water birds tell you?
3. Listen to the song "Pollution" by Tom Lehrer on the record *That Was the Year That Was* (Reprise 6179).
4. How can oysters that live in polluted water spread disease?
5. How are the following materials used to purify water:
   carbon   alum   lime   sand   ozone
   iodine   gravel   chlorine   aluminum sulfate
6. List at least ten ways you use water in your house or apartment.
7. Make a graph to show about how many pints or quarts of water you drink each day.
8. Measure to see how many gallons of water it takes to fill your bathtub.
9. Allow a small amount of tap water to stand in a glass dish until the water evaporates. Is there a white ring left on the dish? What do you think it is from?
10. Does your town have a water pollution control office? If so, find out what it does and how you can help in the fight to end water pollution.
11. Look for editorials and news items in newspapers and magazines that deal with water pollution. Also, look for photographs of the results of water pollution — detergent suds, dead fish, and other problems arising from dirty water.

DATE DUE

OCT 26 2011	

GAYLORD PRINTED IN U.S.A.